Teaching Little Fingers to Christmas Classics

Piano Solos with Optional Teacher Accompaniments

Arranged by
Eric Baumgartner

PLAYBACK+
Speed • Pitch • Balance • Loop

To access audio, visit:
www.halleonard.com/mylibrary

Enter Code
6275-0104-7094-0147

ISBN 978-1-4234-8021-1

WILLIS MUSIC

EXCLUSIVELY DISTRIBUTED BY
HAL•LEONARD®
7777 W. BLUEMOUND RD. P.O. BOX 13819
MILWAUKEE, WISCONSIN 53213

© 2009 by The Willis Music Co.
International Copyright Secured   All Rights Reserved

For all works contained herein:
Unauthorized copying, arranging, adapting, recording, Internet posting, public performance,
or other distribution of the printed or recorded music in this publication is an infringement of copyright.
Infringers are liable under the law.

Visit Hal Leonard Online at
www.halleonard.com

Student Position
One octave higher when performing as a duet

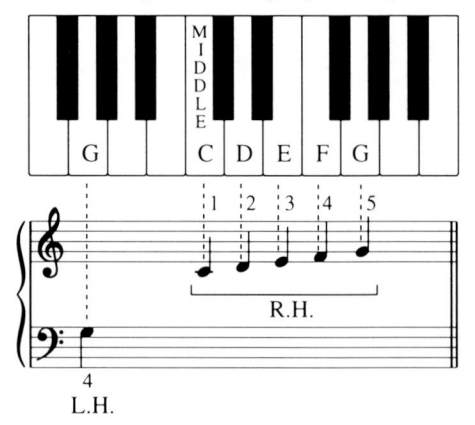

Did You Know?—
Paul McCartney (b. 1942) wrote "Wonderful Christmastime" in 1979. In recent years, contemporary artists such as Hilary Duff, Demi Lovato, and Jars of Clay all recorded versions of the song on their Christmas albums, ensuring its presence in the holiday season for years to come.

Wonderful Christmastime
Optional Teacher Accompaniment

Words and Music by
Paul McCartney
Arranged by Eric Baumgartner

Wonderful Christmastime

Words and Music by
Paul McCartney
Arranged by Eric Baumgartner

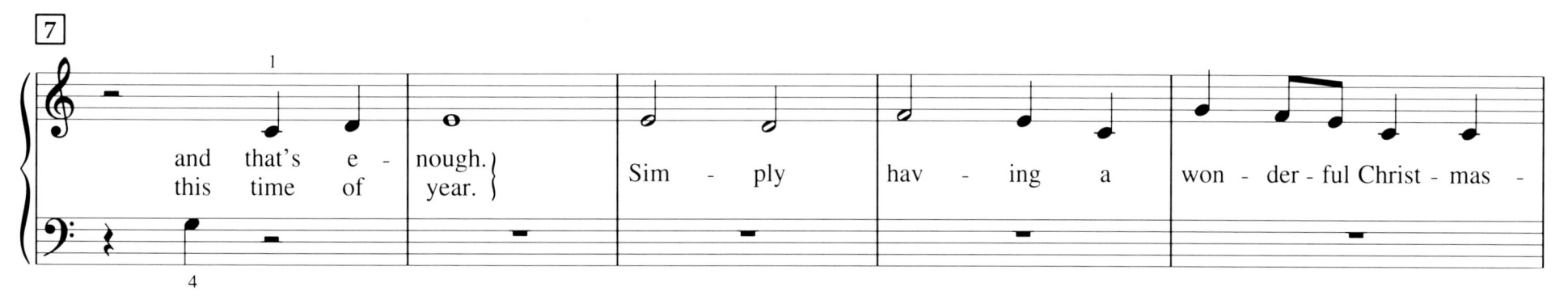

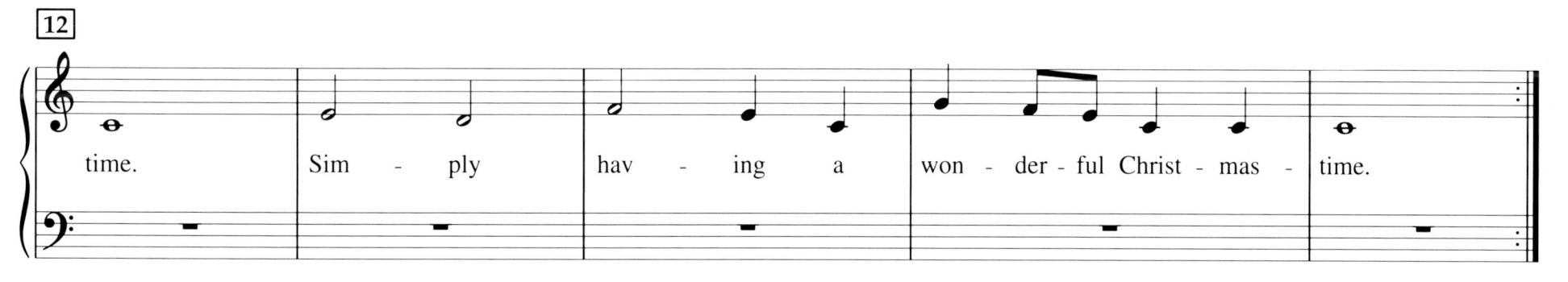

Play both hands one octave higher when performing as a duet.

Brightly

The mood is right, the spir-it's up, we're here to-night,
The par-ty's on, the feel-ing's here that on-ly comes

and that's e-nough. Simply having a wonderful Christmas-
this time of year.

time. Simply having a wonderful Christmastime.

Copyright © 1979 MPL COMMUNICATIONS LTD.
Administered by MPL COMMUNICATIONS, INC.
All Rights Reserved

Student Position
One octave higher when performing as a duet

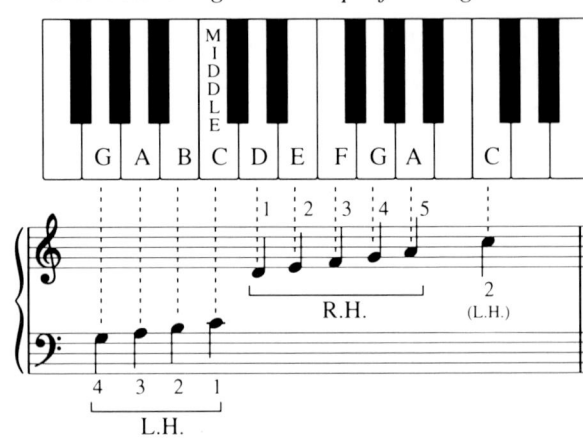

Did You Know?—
"Nuttin' for Christmas" was a hit on the *Billboard* Hot 100 chart in 1955 making a star out of 7-year-old Barry Gordon, who recorded the song with Art Mooney & His Orchestra.

Nuttin' for Christmas
Optional Teacher Accompaniment

Words and Music by Roy Bennett
and Sid Tepper
Arranged by Eric Baumgartner

Nuttin' for Christmas

Words and Music by Roy Bennett
and Sid Tepper
Arranged by Eric Baumgartner

Play both hands one octave higher when performing as a duet.

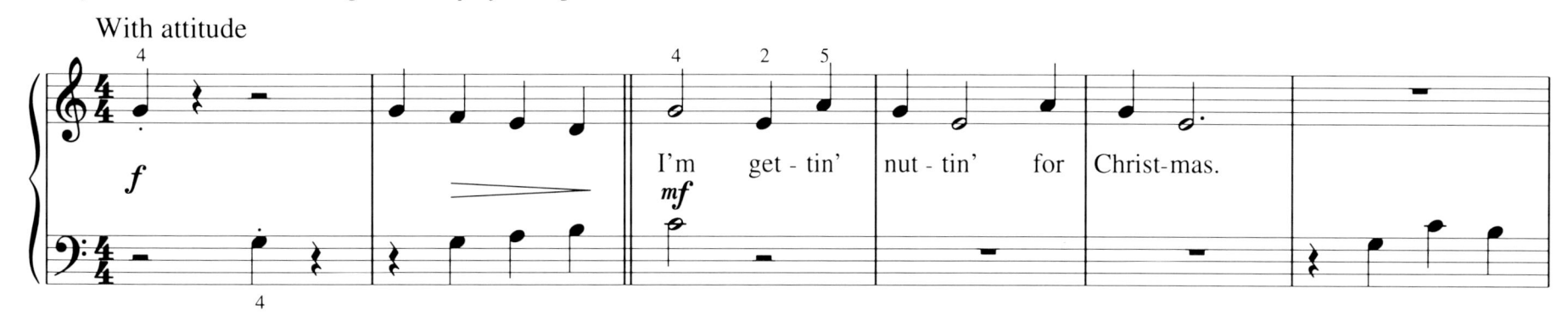

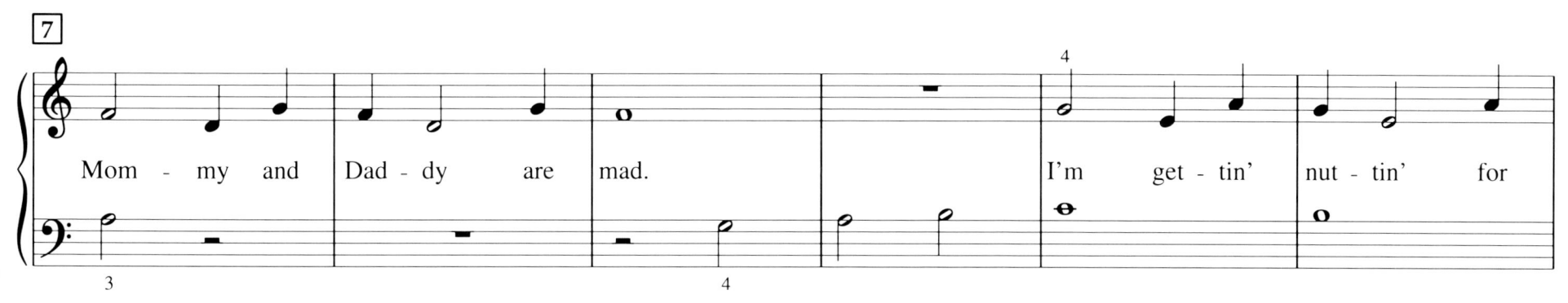

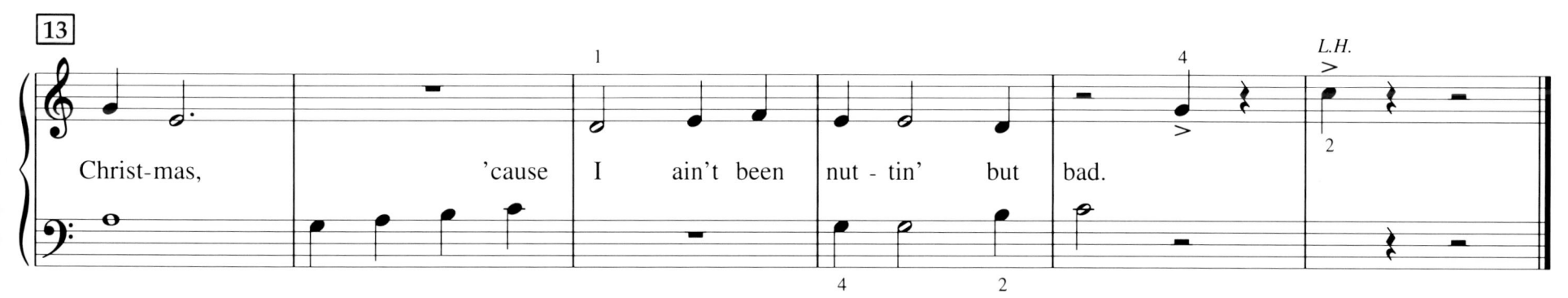

With attitude

I'm get - tin' nut - tin' for Christ - mas.

Mom - my and Dad - dy are mad. I'm get - tin' nut - tin' for

Christ - mas, 'cause I ain't been nut - tin' but bad.

Copyright © 1955 by Chappell & Co.
Copyright Renewed
International Copyright Secured   All Rights Reserved

Student Position
One octave higher when performing as a duet

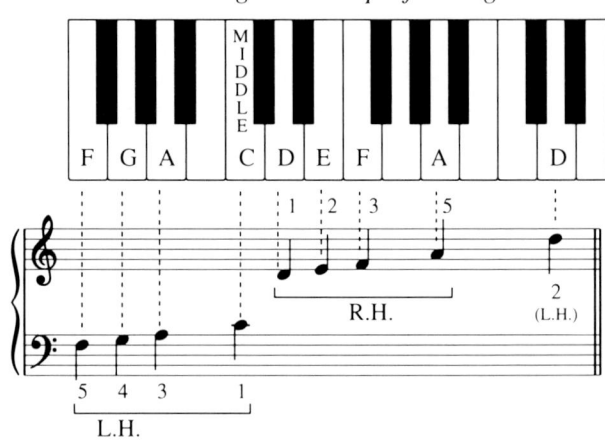

Did You Know?—
John Jacob Niles (1892–1980) was an American composer and singer who would often travel around the country collecting traditional folk songs. In 1933 he discovered fragments of "I Wonder as I Wander" in Appalachian North Carolina, and since then the song has been part of the standard Christmas repertoire. You can find recordings by diverse musicians such as Barbra Streisand, John Rutter and the Cambridge Singers, Julie Andrews, Jewel, and Harry Connick, Jr.

Hint!—
𝄐 is a *fermata*. It means to hold or pause.

I Wonder as I Wander
Optional Teacher Accompaniment

By John Jacob Niles
Arranged by Eric Baumgartner

I Wonder as I Wander

By John Jacob Niles
Arranged by Eric Baumgartner

Play both hands one octave higher when performing as a duet.

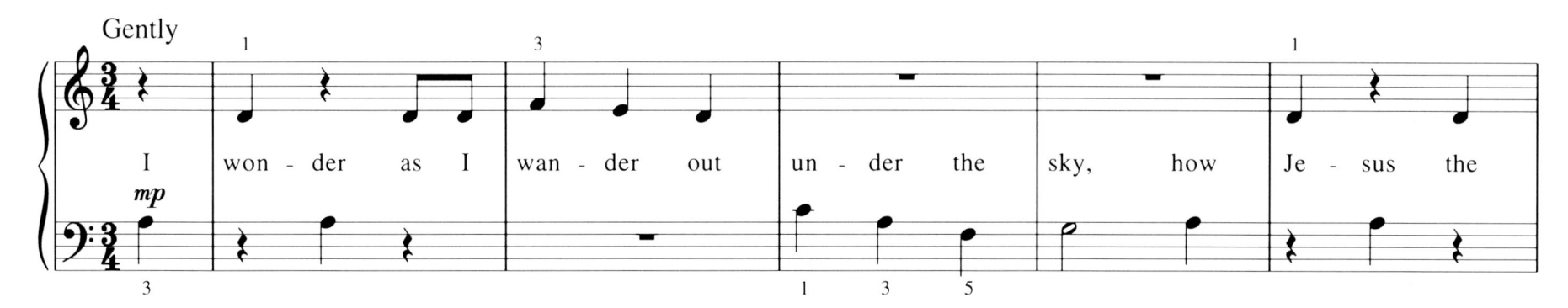

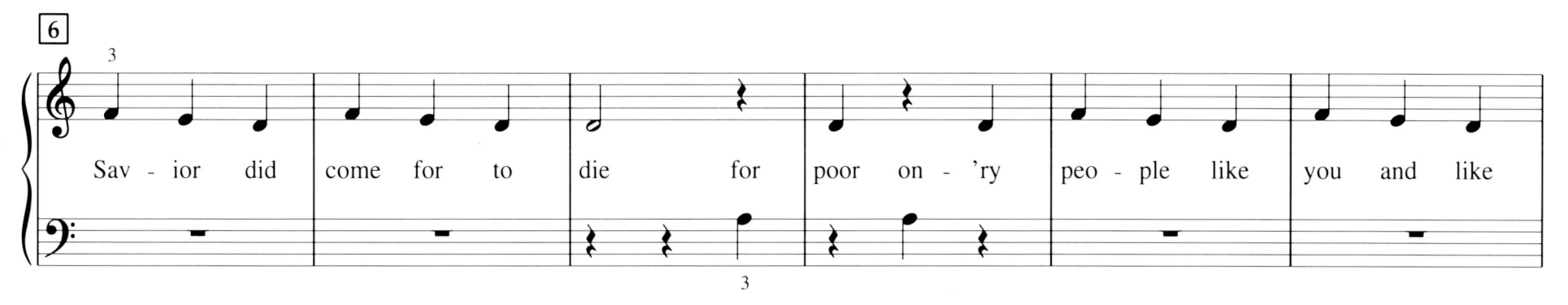

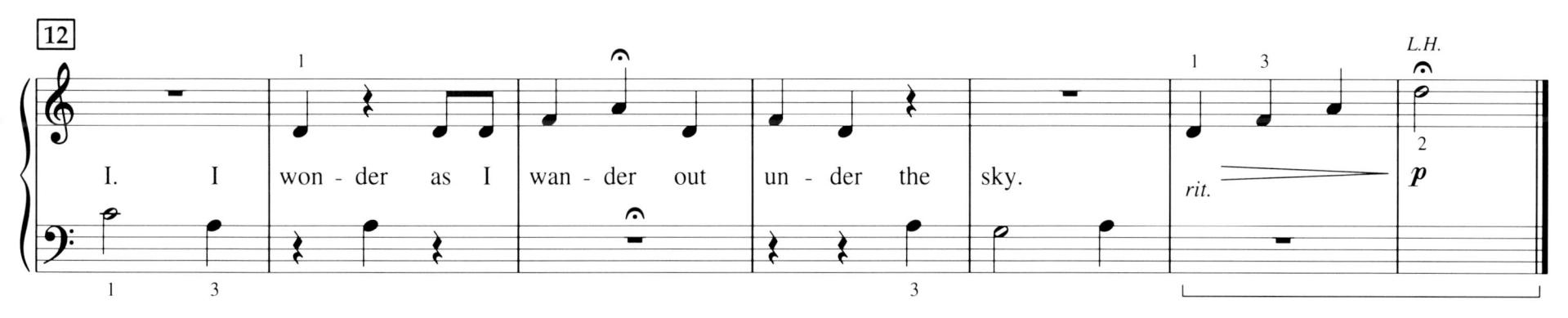

Gently

I won-der as I wan-der out un-der the sky, how Je-sus the Sav-ior did come for to die for poor on-'ry peo-ple like you and like I. I won-der as I wan-der out un-der the sky.

rit.

Copyright © 1934 (Renewed) by G. Schirmer, Inc. (ASCAP), New York, NY
International Copyright Secured   All Rights Reserved
Reprinted by Permission

Did You Know?—
Jester Hairston (1901–2000) was both a composer—he wrote over 300 spirituals—and an actor—he briefly appeared in the films *To Kill a Mockingbird* (1962) and *Being John Malkovich* (1999). "Mary's Little Boy Child" is his best known work—the Harry Belafonte version reached #1 in 1956, as did the Boney M. disco version in 1978.

Student Position
One octave higher when performing as a duet

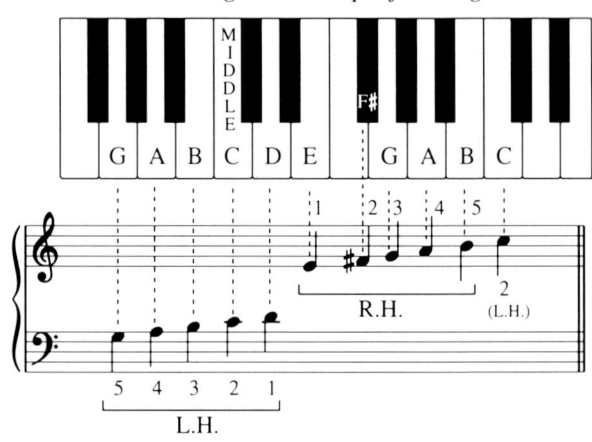

Mary's Little Boy Child
Optional Teacher Accompaniment

Words and Music by
Jester Hairston

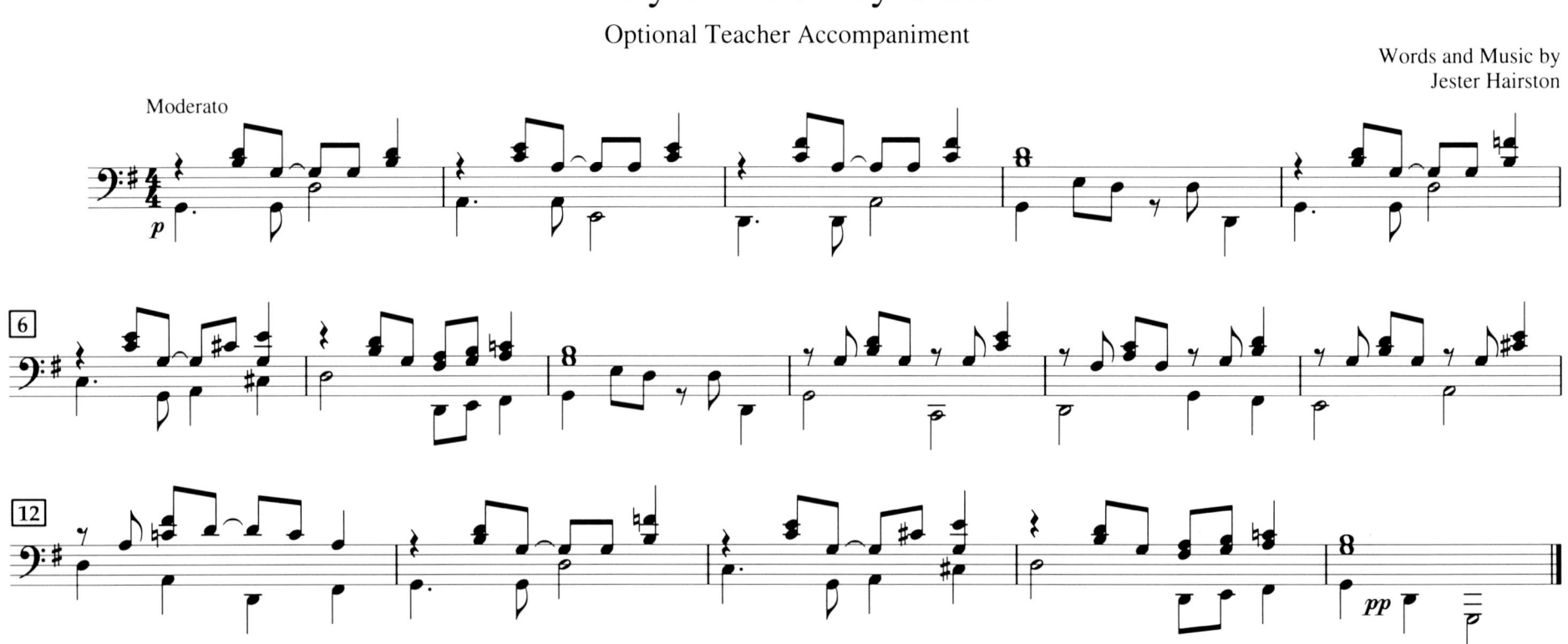

Moderato

Mary's Little Boy Child

Words and Music by
Jester Hairston

Play both hands one octave higher when performing as a duet.

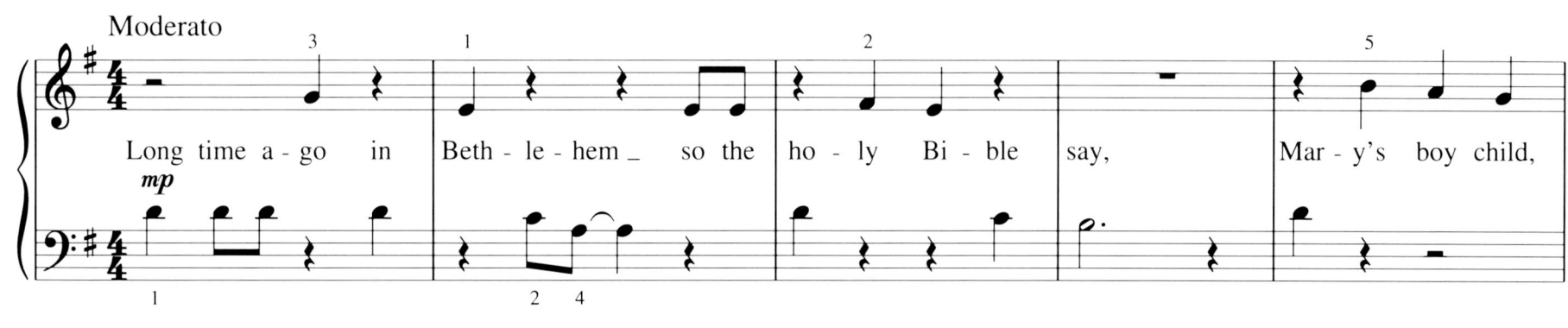

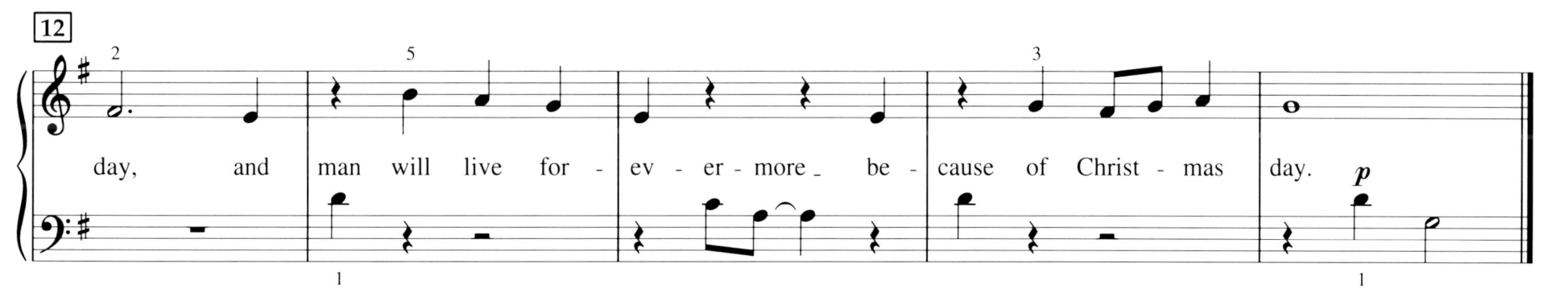

Long time a-go in Beth-le-hem so the ho-ly Bi-ble say, Mar-y's boy child, Je-sus Christ, was born on Christ-mas day. Hark now hear the an-gels sing, new King's born to-day, and man will live for-ev-er-more be-cause of Christ-mas day.

Copyright © 1956 by Schumann Music
Copyright Renewed
All Rights for the World Controlled by Bourne Co.
International Copyright Secured   All Rights Reserved

Did You Know?—
This piece is a very funny novelty Christmas song that became a surprise hit for Elmo Shropshire and his wife Patsy, who originally performed the song in 1979. Mr. Shropshire actually wrote a sequel to it in 2002 called "Grandpa's Gonna Sue the Pants Offa' Santa." (It didn't do as well.)

Hint!—
Be prepared for the hand position change in measure 7.

Student Position
One octave higher when performing as a duet

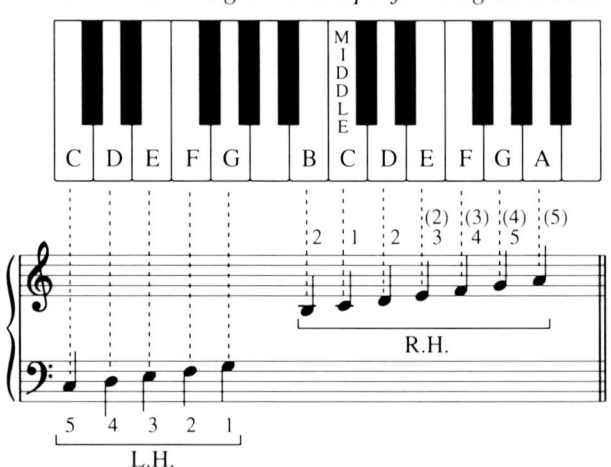

Grandma Got Run Over by a Reindeer
Optional Teacher Accompaniment

Words and Music by
Randy Brooks
Arranged by Eric Baumgartner

Grandma Got Run Over by a Reindeer

Words and Music by
Randy Brooks
Arranged by Eric Baumgartner

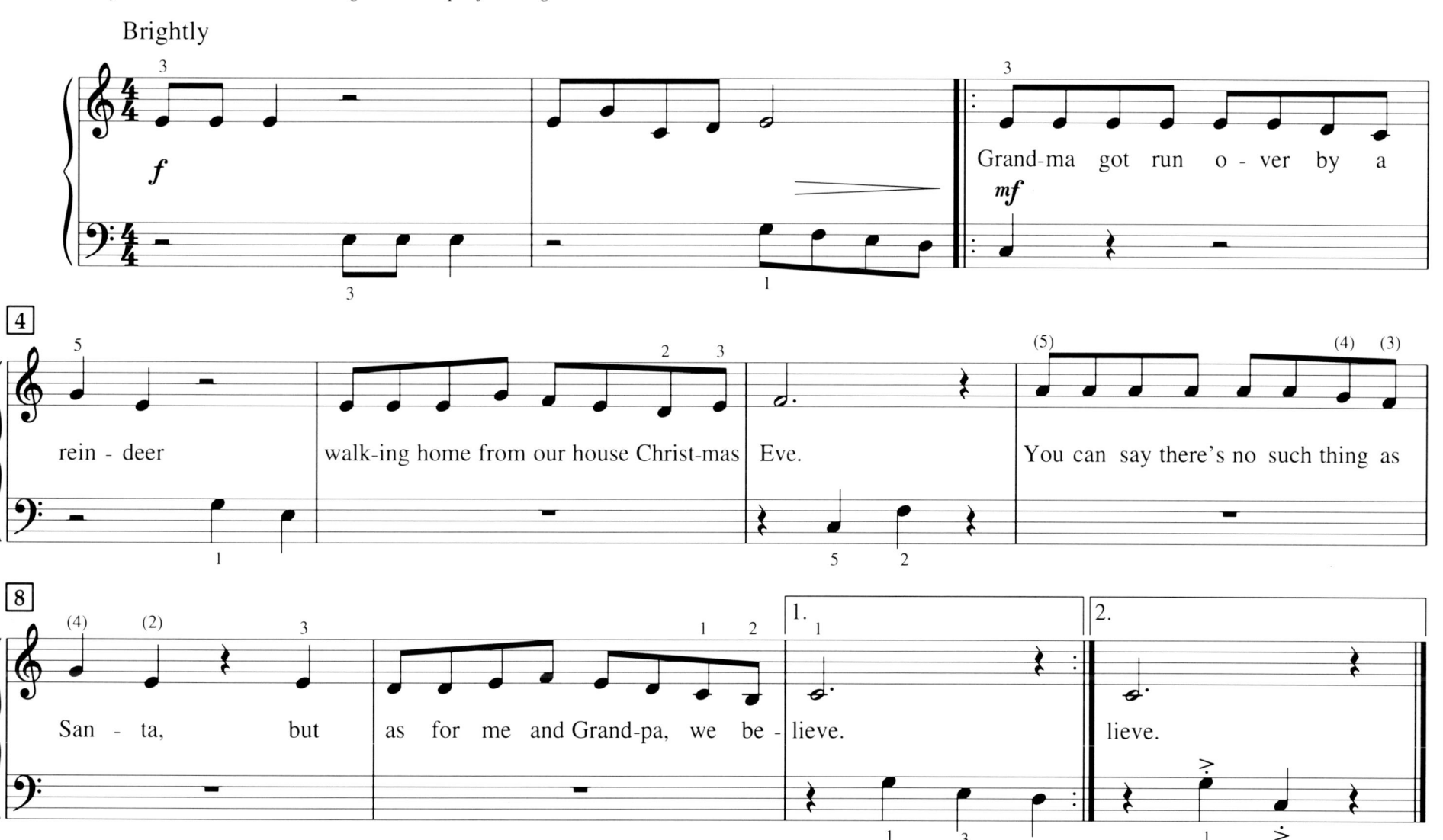

Play both hands one octave higher when performing as a duet.

Grand-ma got run o-ver by a rein-deer walk-ing home from our house Christ-mas Eve. You can say there's no such thing as San-ta, but as for me and Grand-pa, we be-lieve. lieve.

Copyright © 1984 by Kris Publishing (SESAC) and Elmo Publishing (SESAC)
Admin. by ICG
All Rights Reserved   Used by permission

Did You Know?—
"Suzy Snowflake" was popularized by American singer/actress Rosemary Clooney in 1951.

Review—
What key is this piece in?_____
This means the note __ is always flat.

Student Position
One octave higher when performing as a duet

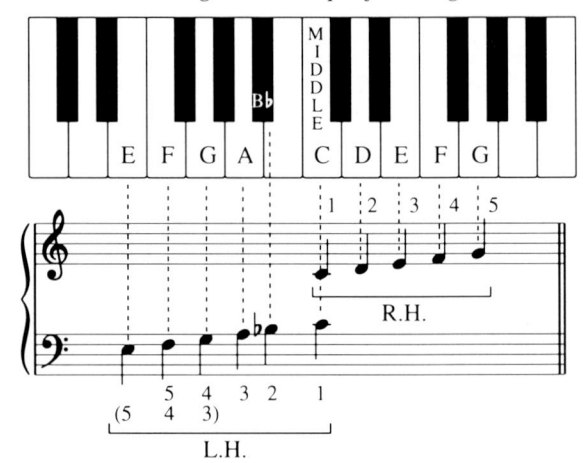

Suzy Snowflake
Optional Teacher Accompaniment

Words and Music by Sid Tepper
and Roy Bennett
Arranged by Eric Baumgartner

Suzy Snowflake

**Words and Music by Sid Tepper
and Roy Bennett**
Arranged by Eric Baumgartner

Play both hands one octave higher when performing as a duet.

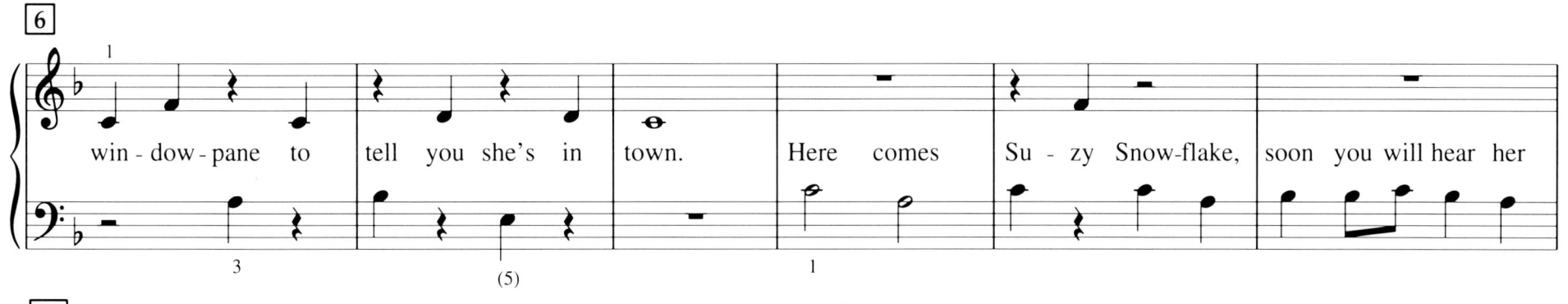

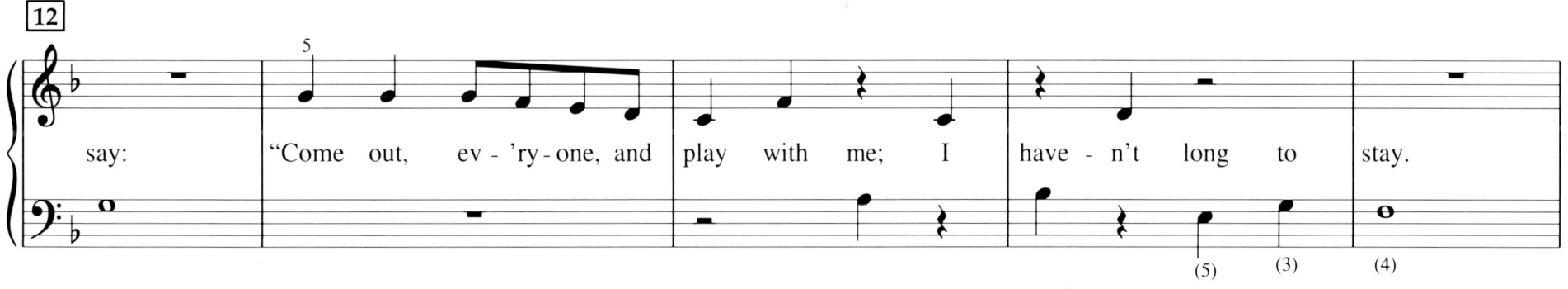

Happily, with a lilt

mf Here comes Su-zy Snow-flake, dressed in a snow-white gown, tap, tap, tap-pin' at your win-dow-pane to tell you she's in town. Here comes Su-zy Snow-flake, soon you will hear her say: "Come out, ev-'ry-one, and play with me; I have-n't long to stay.

Copyright © 1951 by Chappell & Co.
Copyright Renewed
International Copyright Secured   All Rights Reserved

Optional Teacher Accompaniment

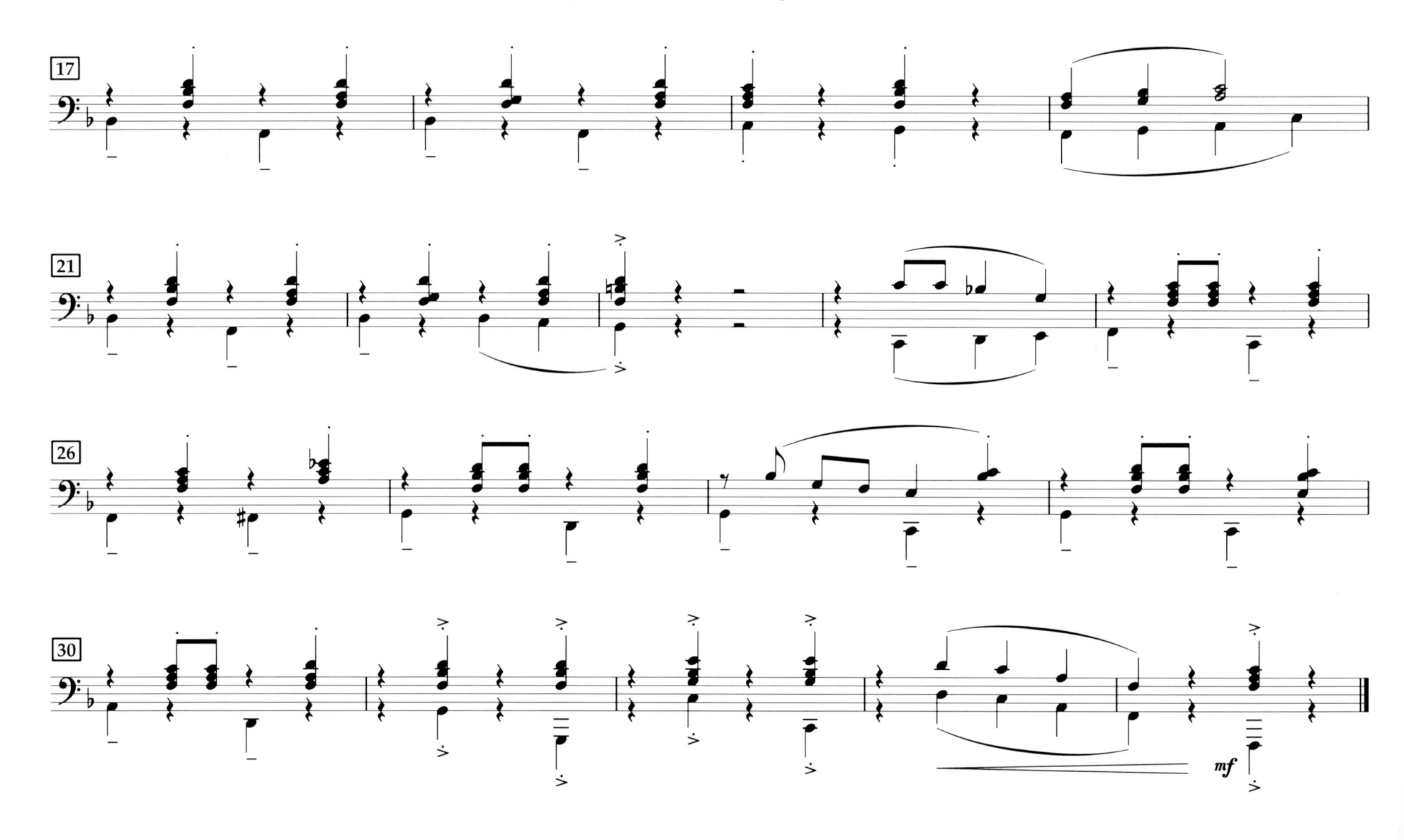

If you wan-na make a snow-man, I'll help you make one. One, two, three! If you wan-na take a sleigh-ride, the ride's on me." Here comes Su-zy Snow-flake, look at her tum-blin' down, bring-ing joy to ev-'ry girl and boy; Su-zy's come to town.

Did You Know?—
Irving Berlin (1888–1989) wrote "White Christmas" while he was basking in the sun by the pool at an Arizona hotel in 1940. The song was used in the movie musical *Holiday Inn* with Bing Crosby and went on to win an Academy Award® for Best Original Song in 1942. It remains one of the best-selling singles of all time—over 100 million copies sold as of this writing!

Hint!—
Take note of the key signature and the extra accidentals sprinkled throughout the piece.

Student Position
One octave higher when performing as a duet

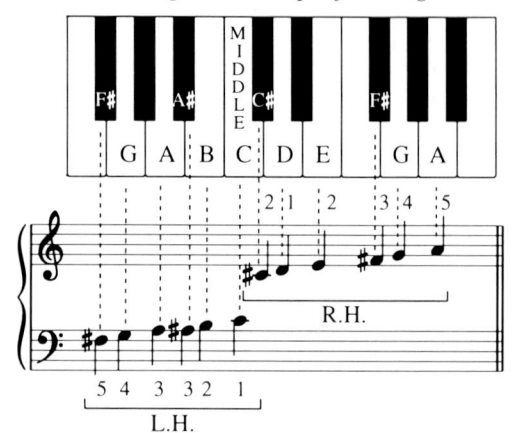

White Christmas
from the Motion Picture Irving Berlin's HOLIDAY INN
Optional Teacher Accompaniment

Words and Music by Irving Berlin
Arranged by Eric Baumgartner

Warmly

With pedal

White Christmas
from the Motion Picture Irving Berlin's HOLIDAY INN

Words and Music by Irving Berlin
Arranged by Eric Baumgartner

Play both hands one octave higher when performing as a duet.

Warmly

I'm dreaming of a white Christmas, just like the ones I used to know, where the treetops glisten and children listen to

© Copyright 1940, 1942 by Irving Berlin
Copyright Renewed
International Copyright Secured All Rights Reserved

Optional Teacher Accompaniment

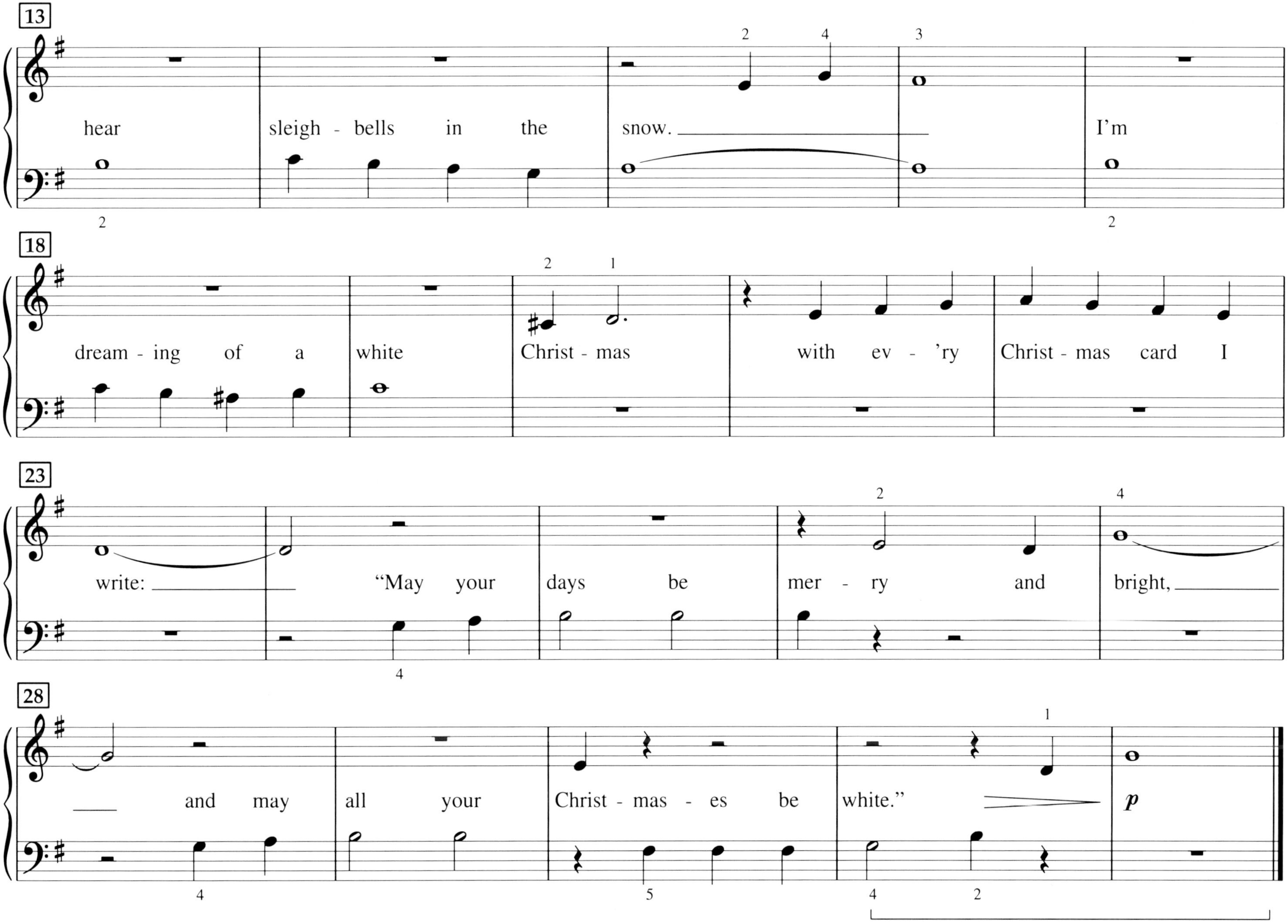
13
hear sleigh - bells in the snow. I'm
18
dream - ing of a white Christ - mas with ev - 'ry Christ - mas card I
23
write: "May your days be mer - ry and bright,
28
and may all your Christ - mas - es be white."
p

Johnny Marks (1909–1985) was a prolific Christmas songwriter. His most popular tune is "Rudolph the Red-Nosed Reindeer." Mr. Marks also served as director of the American Society of Composers, Authors and Publishers (ASCAP) from 1957–1961.

Hint!—
"Jingle, Jingle, Jingle" has a few more hand position changes than usual—especially in the left hand!—so pay close attention.

Jingle, Jingle, Jingle
Optional Teacher Accompaniment

Music and Lyrics by Johnny Marks
Arranged by Eric Baumgartner

Jingle, Jingle, Jingle

Music and Lyrics by Johnny Marks
Arranged by Eric Baumgartner

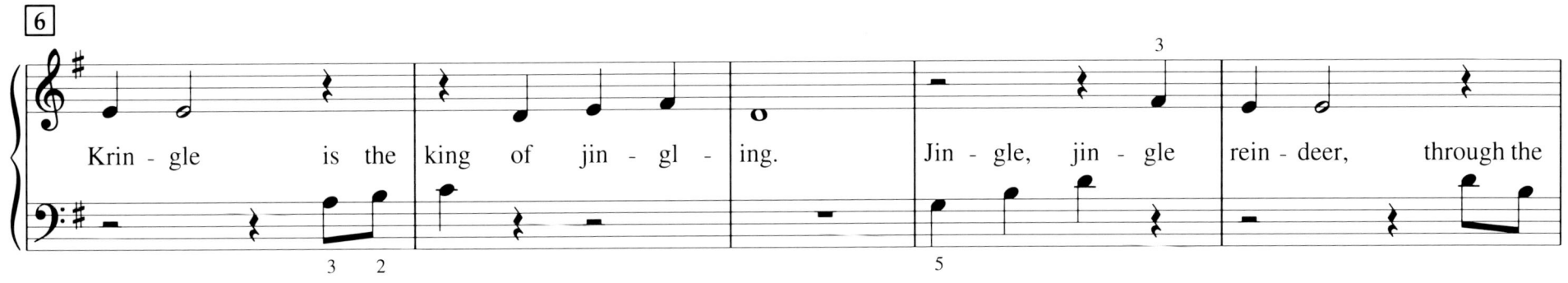

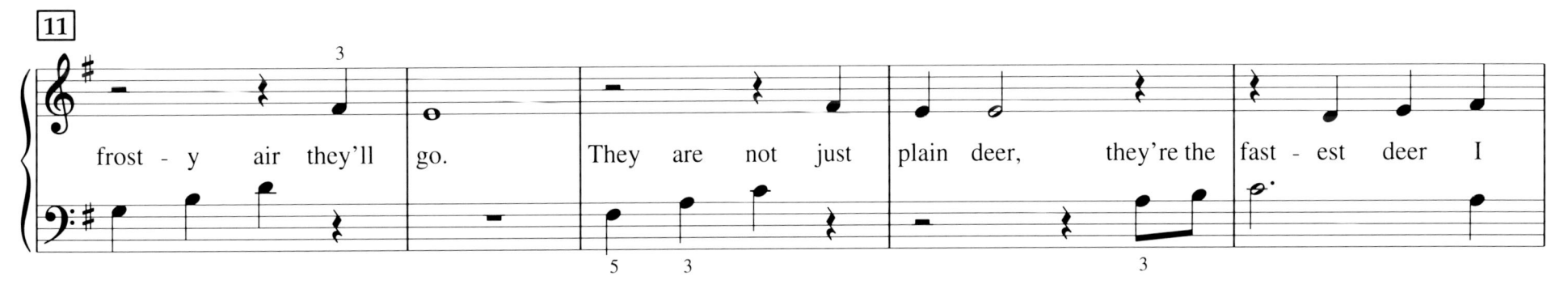

Play both hands one octave higher when performing as a duet.

Merrily

Jin - gle, jin - gle, jin - gle, you will hear his sleigh-bells ring, Jol - ly old Kris Krin - gle is the king of jin - gl - ing. Jin - gle, jin - gle rein - deer, through the frost - y air they'll go. They are not just plain deer, they're the fast - est deer I

Copyright © 1964 (Renewed 1992) St. Nicholas Music Inc., 1619 Broadway, New York, New York 10019
All Rights Reserved

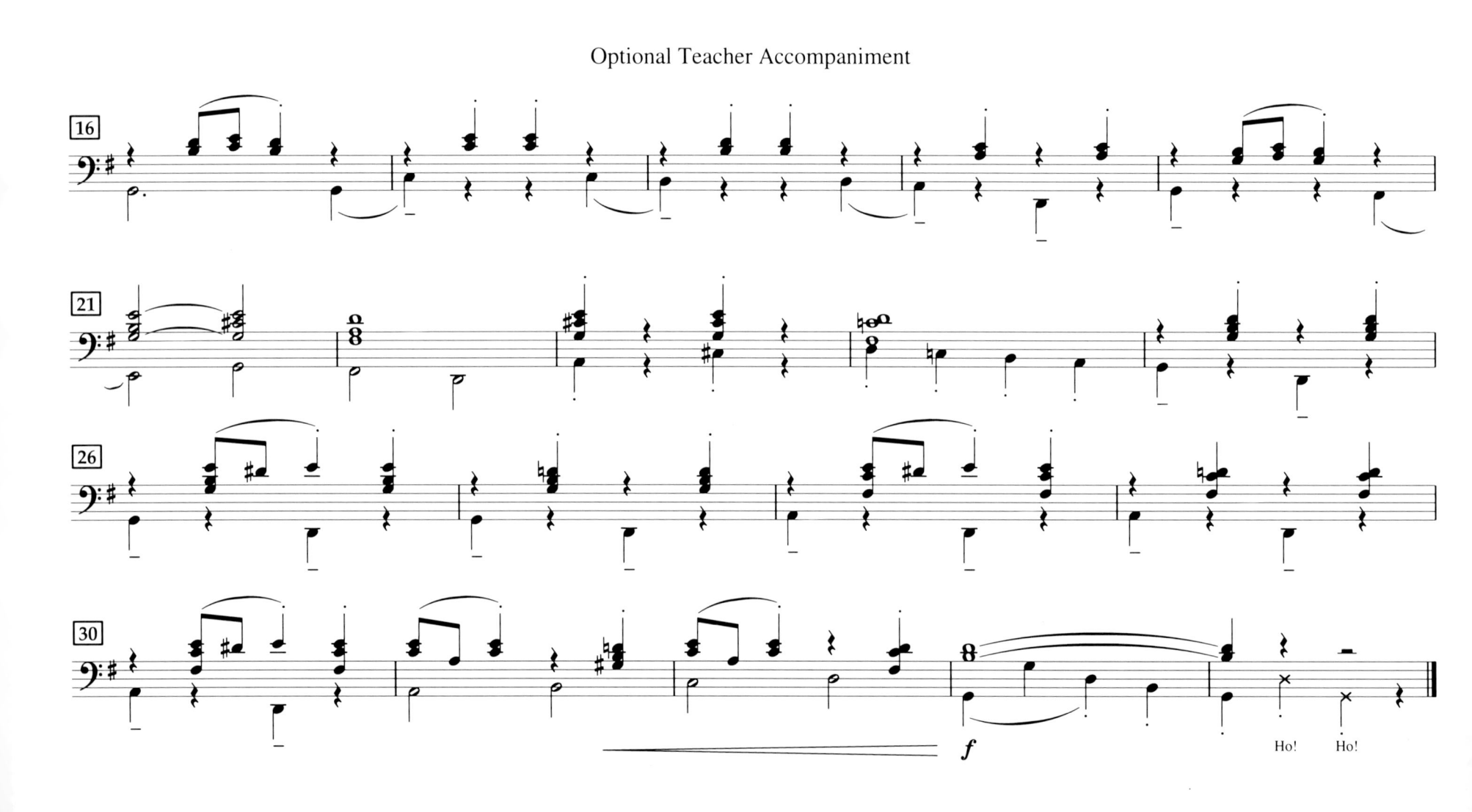

Optional Teacher Accompaniment

16
know. You must be - lieve that on Christ - mas Eve he won't pass you by. He'll
21
dash a - way in his mag - ic sleigh, fly - ing through the sky. Jin - gle, jin - gle,
26
jin - gle, you will hear his sleigh - bells ring, Jol - ly old Kris
30
Krin - gle is the king of jin - gl - ing.
f

TEACHING LITTLE FINGERS TO PLAY

TEACHING LITTLE FINGERS TO PLAY
by John Thompson

A series for the early beginner combining rote and note approach. The melodies are written with careful thought and are kept as simple as possible, yet they are refreshingly delightful. All the music lies within the grasp of the child's small hands.

00412076 Book only $5.99
00406523 Book/Audio..............................$9.99

TEACHING LITTLE FINGERS TO PLAY ENSEMBLE
by John Thompson

A book of intermediate-level accompaniments for use in the teacher's studio or at home. Two possible accompaniments are included for each *Teaching Little Fingers* piece: a Secondo or Primo part, as well as a second piano part for studios that have two pianos/keyboards.

00412228 Book only $5.99

DISNEY TUNES
arr. Glenda Austin

10 delightful Disney songs: The Bare Necessities • Can You Feel the Love Tonight • Candle on the Water • God Help the Outcasts • Kiss the Girl • Mickey Mouse March • The Siamese Cat Song • Winnie the Pooh • You'll Be in My Heart (Pop Version) • Zip-A-Dee-Doo-Dah.

00416748 Book only $9.99
00416749 Book/Audio.............................$12.99

CHRISTMAS CAROLS
arr. Carolyn Miller

12 piano solos: Angels We Have Heard on High • Deck the Hall • The First Noel • Hark! The Herald Angels Sing • Jingle Bells • Jolly Old Saint Nicholas • Joy to the World! • O Come, All Ye Faithful • O Come Little Children • Silent Night • Up on the Housetop • We Three Kings of Orient Are.

00406391 Book only $6.99
00406722 Book/Audio............................$10.99

CLASSICS
arr. Randall Hartsell

11 piano classics: Bridal Chorus (from *Lohengrin*) (Wagner) • Can-Can (from *Orpheus in the Underworld*) (Offenbach) • Country Gardens (English Folk Tune) • A Little Night Music (from *Eine kleine Nachtmusik*) (Mozart) • Lullaby (Brahms) • Ode to Joy (from Symphony No. 9) (Beethoven) • Symphony No. 5 (Second Movement) (Tchaikovsky) • and more.

00406550 Book only $6.99
00406736 Book/Audio............................$10.99

HYMNS
arr. Mary K. Sallee

11 hymns: Amazing Grace • Faith of Our Fathers • For the Beauty of the Earth • Holy, Holy, Holy • Jesus Loves Me • Jesus Loves the Little Children • Joyful, Joyful, We Adore Thee • Kum Bah Yah • Praise Him, All Ye Little Children • We Are Climbing Jacob's Ladder • What a Friend We Have in Jesus.

00406413 Book only $5.99
00406731 Book/Audio............................$10.99

TEACHING LITTLE FINGERS TO PLAY MORE
by Leigh Kaplan

Teaching Little Fingers to Play More is a fun-filled and colorfully illustrated follow-up book to *Teaching Little Fingers to Play*. This book strengthens skills learned while easing the transition into John Thompson's *Modern Course, Book One*.

00406137 Book only $6.99
00406527 Book/Audio..............................$9.99

MORE DISNEY TUNES
arr. Glenda Austin

9 songs, including: Circle of Life • Colors of the Wind • A Dream Is a Wish Your Heart Makes • A Spoonful of Sugar • Under the Sea • A Whole New World • and more.

00416750 Book only $9.99
00416751 Book/Audio............................$12.99

MORE EASY DUETS
arr. Carolyn Miller

9 more fun duets arranged for 1 piano, 4 hands: A Bicycle Built for Two (Daisy Bell) • Blow the Man Down • Chopsticks • Do Your Ears Hang Low? • I've Been Working on the Railroad • The Man on the Flying Trapeze • Short'nin' Bread • Skip to My Lou • The Yellow Rose of Texas.

00416832 Book only $6.99
00416833 Book/Audio............................$10.99

MORE BROADWAY SONGS
arr. Carolyn Miller

10 more fantastic Broadway favorites arranged for a young performer, including: Castle on a Cloud • Climb Ev'ry Mountain • Gary, Indiana • In My Own Little Corner • It's the Hard-Knock Life • Memory • Oh, What a Beautiful Mornin' • Sunrise, Sunset • Think of Me • Where Is Love?

00416928 Book only $6.99
00416929 Book/Audio............................$12.99

MORE CHILDREN'S SONGS
arr. by Carolyn Miller

10 songs: The Candy Man • Do-Re-Mi • I'm Popeye the Sailor Man • It's a Small World • Linus and Lucy • The Muppet Show Theme • My Favorite Things • Sesame Street Theme • Supercalifragilisticexpialidocious • Tomorrow.

00416810 Book only $6.99
00416811 Book/Audio............................$12.99

EXCLUSIVELY DISTRIBUTED BY
WILLIS MUSIC / HAL•LEONARD

Prices, contents, and availability subject to change without notice.
Disney characters and artwork © Disney Enterprises, Inc.

All arrangements come with optional teacher accompaniments.

FOR A COMPLETE SERIES LISTING, VISIT WWW.HALLEONARD.COM